The CHRISTMAS Book

Rita Storey

A⁺
Smart Apple Media

Published by Smart Apple Media,
an imprint of Black Rabbit Books
P.O. Box 3263, Mankato, Minnesota 56002
www.blackrabbitbooks.com

Printed in the United States
of America at Worzalla,
Stevens Point, Wisconsin.

Published by arrangement with the Watts
Publishing Group LTD, London.

Editor: Paul Rockett
Design: Ruth Walton
Picture Research: Diana Morris
Illustrator: Shelagh McNicholas, pp 8-11
Commissioned photography: Paul Bricknell
    Photography, pp13, 17, 19, 20-3, 26-7,
    30, 32-3, 35

Library of Congress Cataloging-in-Publication Data

Storey, Rita.
The Christmas Book / Rita Storey.
pages cm-(Seasonal companions)
Includes index.
ISBN 978-1-59920-957-9
1. Christmas--Juvenile literature. I. Title.
GT4985.5.S76 2015
394.2663--dc23   2013033655

PO1656
Date: 4-2014

9 8 7 6 5 4 3 2 1

Every attempt has been made to clear copyright. Should there be any inadvertent omission please apply to the publisher for rectification.

Picture credits:
abimages/Shutterstock: 28cl; AGfoto/Shutterstock: 31c; andere/Shutterstock: front cover tr, 18b, 24b, 25b, 45t; Anteromite/Shutterstock: front cover tcr, 18cr, 44t; Art Directors/Alamy: 42-43; Atlaspix/Shutterstock: 29cl inset; bildagenteur-online/begsteiger/Alamy: 8c; Borderlands/Alamy: 14c; c/Shutterstock? 29cr inset; Valeria Cantone/Dreamstime: 37t; Paul Cowan/Shutterstock: 29cr; Cubo Images/Superstock: 36c; Sandra Cunningham/Shutterstock: 16c; Chad Ehlers/Alamy: 15t; Eliks/Shutterstock: 26tr; Elena Elisseeva/Shutterstock: 29tl; Gert Ellstrom/Shutterstock: 21b; evarin20/Shutterstock: front cover br, 26tl, 45br; Fenton/Shutterstock: 28cl inset; Fotogroove/Shutterstock: 28tl inset; Nicole Gordine/Shutterstock: 14b; granata1111/Shutterstock: 28bl; Spencer Grant/Alamy: 7tl; Brian Harris/Alamy: 38t, 38b, 38b, 41b; Steve Heap/Shutterstock: 34tl; Svetlana Ivanova/Shutterstock: 3-4, 22-23 bg, 30-31bg, 40-41 bg, 46-47 bg; joingate/Shutterstock: 25c; Joyfuldesigns/Dreamstime: 8t; Daniel Karman/dpa/Corbis: 15b; Teresa Kasprzycka/Shutterstock: 28tl; kbecca/Shutterstock: 26-27 bg, 35bg, 38-39bg, 44-45 bg; Tatiana Kitaeva/Shutterstock: 28cr; Nigel Monkton/Dreamstime: 29br; mountainpix/Shutterstock: 24cr; National Archives, London/Mary Evans PL: 34; Nicemonkey/Shutterstock: 28cr inset; Madeleine Openshaw/Shutterstock: 37c; Marcin Pawlinski/Dreamstime: 6b; pearl7/Shutterstock: 29 cl; Dusan Po/Shutterstock: 29br inset; ratselmeister/Shutterstock: 1-2, 13bg, 20-21 bg, 31b, 32-33 bg, 48-49 bg; Stephen Aaron Rees/Shutterstock: 29 tl inset; Jim Ringland/Art Directors/Alamy: 7cr; Luis Santos/Shutterstock: front cover tcl, 6t; Seth Solesbee/Shutterstock: 18cl; Paula Solloway/Alamy: 7tr; Sorge/Caro/Alamy: 7cl; Tanor/Shutterstock: front cover bl, 24t; Alfonso de Thomas/Dreamstime: 36b; tratong/Shutterstock: 28br; Wikimedia Commons: 25t; Peter Wollanga/Dreamstime: 6c; Yakobina/Shutterstock: 24cl; Naci Yavuz/Shutterstock: 36-37 bg; yienkeat/Shutterstock: 8b, 14t.

Contents

What is Christmas?

Christmas Day is on December 25. It is a festival celebrated by millions of people all over the world. But why? Where does it come from?

Midwinter celebrations

People held midwinter celebrations a long time before anyone had heard of Christmas. People used to worship nature as they relied on the seasons to bring the sunshine and the rain to grow their crops and feed their animals. These people were called pagans. There were lots of midwinter festivals.

In England a festival was held on the shortest day of the year (the winter solstice). It reminded everyone that after the long nights of winter, the sunshine and light would return.

In Scandinavia the festival was called "Yule" and a log was burned to celebrate the return of the light.

The Romans held a festival called "saturnalia" to honor the god Saturn, the god of agriculture and harvest.

Celebrating the birth of Jesus

Christmas today comes from the celebration of the birth of baby Jesus. No one really knows when Jesus was born. The Bible does not give us any clues. Some people believe

that it was the Roman emperor Constantine who merged some of the pagan winter festivals with the early Christian celebrations of the birth of Jesus. Constantine had converted to Christianity and wanted everyone to celebrate the birth of Jesus. He set a date for the celebration of Christ's mass or Christmas right in the middle of winter, so that if the pagan celebrations remained they could be given a new Christian meaning.

How do you celebrate Christmas?

These children are taking part in various Christmas activities.
People celebrate Christmas in different ways around the world.
Which part of Christmas do you enjoy most?

The real meaning of Christmas

It may seem as though Christmas celebrations today have little to do with the story of the birth of Jesus all those years ago. Most people celebrate Christmas by sending cards and giving presents. They may decorate a Christmas tree with lights and put an angel or a star on top. Some might hang a wreath on the front door. In fact, these things are all symbols of the real meaning of Christmas. Find out more throughout this book.

The Christmas Story

The Christmas story tells us about the birth of Jesus.

Once, about 2,000 years ago, a young woman named Mary lived in a town called Nazareth. She was engaged to be married to a young man named Joseph. One night, an angel appeared to Mary and told her that God had chosen her for a very special purpose. She was to be the mother of God's son on Earth, and she must call him Jesus. Mary felt great joy at the news.

At first, Joseph didn't believe Mary's news. Then an angel appeared to him and told him that it was true. Soon after the angel's visit, Mary and Joseph were married.

Mary's baby was nearly due when a letter arrived ordering everybody to return to their birthplace. The Romans, who ruled the land, wanted to count all the people and collect their taxes.

Joseph and Mary had
to travel to Joseph's
home town of
Bethlehem. It was
a long journey.
They had to travel
for days, over open
plains and across
mountains, with
only a single donkey
to carry them.

They slept on the
ground and stopped
at villages to eat whatever
they could find. As they
reached Bethlehem, Mary
realized it was almost time for
the baby to be born.

Frantically Joseph searched
for somewhere to stay, but everywhere
he found was full. Finally, an innkeeper
took pity on the couple and offered them a stable
at the back of his inn. Sheep and cattle were kept there, but
it was warm and dry. So, exhausted from the journey, Joseph
made Mary as comfortable as he could in the stable.

That night, Mary gave birth to a baby boy and wrapped him in swaddling clothes. She placed him in a manger as a makeshift crib. Meanwhile, in the fields outside Bethlehem, some shepherds huddled around a fire, keeping watch over their sheep. Suddenly, an angel appeared before them.

At first they were frightened, but the angel told them news of the birth of baby Jesus. They were excited to be the first to know.

As Mary and Joseph rested in the stable with baby Jesus, they were startled by the shepherds' appearance. The shepherds had come to see if the angel's words were true. As soon as they saw baby Jesus, they knelt down before him.

At the same time, a bright star appeared in the sky above Bethlehem. Three kings saw the star and set out to follow it. On the way they went to a palace that belonged to King Herod. They told Herod that the star was a sign that a new king had been born. Herod pretended to be pleased, but he was secretly angry. He feared a more important king than him might have been born. He asked the wise men to return and tell him where the baby king could be found.

The three kings followed the star to Bethlehem, where they found Jesus. They worshipped him and gave him gifts of gold, frankincense, and myrrh.

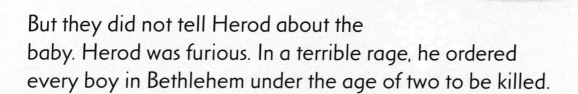

But they did not tell Herod about the baby. Herod was furious. In a terrible rage, he ordered every boy in Bethlehem under the age of two to be killed.

An angel appeared and told Joseph of the danger. He, Mary, and Jesus fled at once to Egypt. The family stayed there until, one day, they heard news of Herod's death. At last it was safe for them to return to Nazareth.

All About Advent

The time before Christmas is called Advent. Advent begins on the fourth Sunday before Christmas and lasts until Christmas Eve. When Christians go to church on these four Sundays they remember the events leading up to Jesus' birth.

Advent wreath

Some churches have an advent wreath made of evergreen leaves with five candles. There are four candles around the outside that stand for hope, peace, love, and joy, and a white one in the center that represents Jesus as the light of the world. The outside candles are lit on the four Sundays of Advent, and the white one on Christmas Day.

Advent calendars

Although the period of Advent can begin before December, most people start counting down to Christmas from December 1. Many do this with an advent calendar. An advent calendar has 24 doors, one to open each day in December before Christmas Day. Behind each door is a picture or even a chocolate treat.

Light of the world

Jesus is often called "the light of the world". For Christians, lighting candles and putting up lights at Christmastime is a sign that Jesus was born to give the world hope.

Christmas numbers!

There are 24 doors on an advent calendar. Do you know any more Christmas numbers? What numbers are missing below?

- X days of Christmas
- X candles in an advent crown
- X wise men
- Santa Claus has X reindeer.

Answers on page 44

Make an advent calendar

You can make your own advent calendar. It could be made personal by using photographs. Use a selection showing family, friends, pets and pictures of favorite places.

You can also cut out images from last year's Christmas cards. Any picture smaller than the size of a matchbox will work.

You will need:
❋ **2 sheets tagboard**
❋ **matchbox and pencil**
❋ **glue and spatula**
❋ **craft knife**
❋ **24 pictures to go behind the windows**

Instructions

1. On one sheet of tagboard, draw round the matchbox 24 times.

2. Ask an adult to cut along the top and bottom lines of each rectangle with a craft knife. Then cut a line down the center of the rectangle, from top to bottom (an H-shape on its side).

3. Carefully spread glue on the entire piece of tagboard except inside the cutout shapes.

4. Glue the piece of card with cutout shapes to the second piece of tagboard.

5. Fold back the flaps of each shape. Glue your pictures on the backing board underneath the window flaps. Then leave to dry.

6. Press the flaps back in place. Decorate the front of the card and write the numbers 1 to 24 on the windows.

Get Ready for Christmas

From the beginning of December, or even earlier, it is impossible to forget that Christmas is getting close. Everywhere there are Christmas lights and decorations, carols being played and Christmas songs being sung. In some countries, the time leading up to Christmas has very special celebrations.

Posada

In Mexico, from December 16 to Christmas Eve, people often take part in Posada (lodgings) processions. These act out the part of the Christmas story where Joseph and Mary looked for a room in Bethlehem. Children carry a statue of Mary and Joseph.

The children call at the houses of friends and neighbours and sing a song about Joseph and Mary asking for a room in the house. They are told that there is no room and to go away. After visiting a few houses they are told there is room and are welcomed in to a Posada party.

St. Nicholas's Day

St. Nicholas's Day is December 6 (see page 24). In many countries in Europe, as well as parts of the US and Canada, it is the main day for giving presents. Children leave out shoes or stockings and, if they have been good, St. Nicholas fills them with presents.

St. Lucia's Day

In some European countries, including Sweden, Denmark, Norway, and Finland, December 13 is St. Lucia's Day. St. Lucia was a brave young girl who was killed because she was a Christian. On St. Lucia's Day, a girl leads a procession of people singing carols. She wears a white dress with a red sash round her waist and a crown of evergreen leaves and candles on her head. St. Lucia's Day buns, called *lussekatts*, are eaten in Scandinavia for breakfast. These are raisin buns flavored with saffron.

In some parts of Italy, children leave out a sandwich for St. Lucia and her donkey as a thank you for the gifts that they receive on St. Lucia's Day.

Christkind

In Germany, the *Christkind* is described as a young girl with "Christlike" qualities. In Nürnberg, a young girl is chosen every year to be in a parade as the *Christkind*. She wears a long white and gold dress, has long blond, curly hair and wears a gold crown and sometimes wings like an angel.

15

Christmas Cards

Many people send and receive Christmas cards each year. It's a great way of staying in touch with people you may not have seen or heard from all year — and a great way to spread Christmas cheer!

A short history

The tradition of exchanging written greetings goes back to both the ancient Chinese and the ancient Egyptians, but the first Christmas cards did not appear until 1846. They were the idea of Henry Cole, the first director of the Victoria and Albert Museum in London. Only 1,000 cards were produced — they were very expensive and were not a great success. In 1860, a new printing process was introduced that meant the cards could be produced at a lower cost. This, along with inexpensive postage rates, meant that the idea really took off.

CHRISTMAS CARD FACTS

Each year, more than 1.5 billion Christmas cards are sent in the US alone.

An average American household will send 20 Christmas cards and receive 20 in their place.

Christmas cards make up 60% of seasonal card sales each year.

Christmas card making is one of the most popular craft hobbies in the US.

ECO TIP

Do not put your used cards in the wastebasket! Either recycle them or, better yet, keep them until next year and re-use them as gift tags.
To use them as gift tags: cut out the pictures into the shape of the tag you want. Make a hole with a hole punch and thread with string or ribbon through the hole.
To turn them into new cards: fold a piece of blank card in half. Glue the picture on to the front — decorate with ribbon, glitter, and sequins and write a new greeting inside.

Make thumbprint cards

Turn your thumbprints into reindeers, robins, trees, snowmen and lots of other Christmassy things.

Instructions

1. Fold the cardstock in half.

2. Squeeze a blob of paint onto the saucer.

3. Dip your thumb in the paint.

4. On the scrap paper make some thumbprints to remove any extra paint.

5. Make a thumbprint on the cardstock and let dry.

6. To turn your thumbprint into a **reindeer**, add a nose (red for Rudolf!) antlers, legs, and eyes, using the felt-tip pens. To turn your thumbprint into a **robin**, add a beak, wings, and feet. To turn your thumbprint into a **snowman**, add a nose, eyes, and arms.

Put your card in an envelope and mail it to a friend... Don't forget the stamp!

You will need:

* ❊ **a piece of cardstock twice the final width of your card** (to fit in an envelope if you wish to mail it)
* ❊ **poster paints**
* ❊ **saucer**
* ❊ **scrap paper**
* ❊ **felt-tip pens**

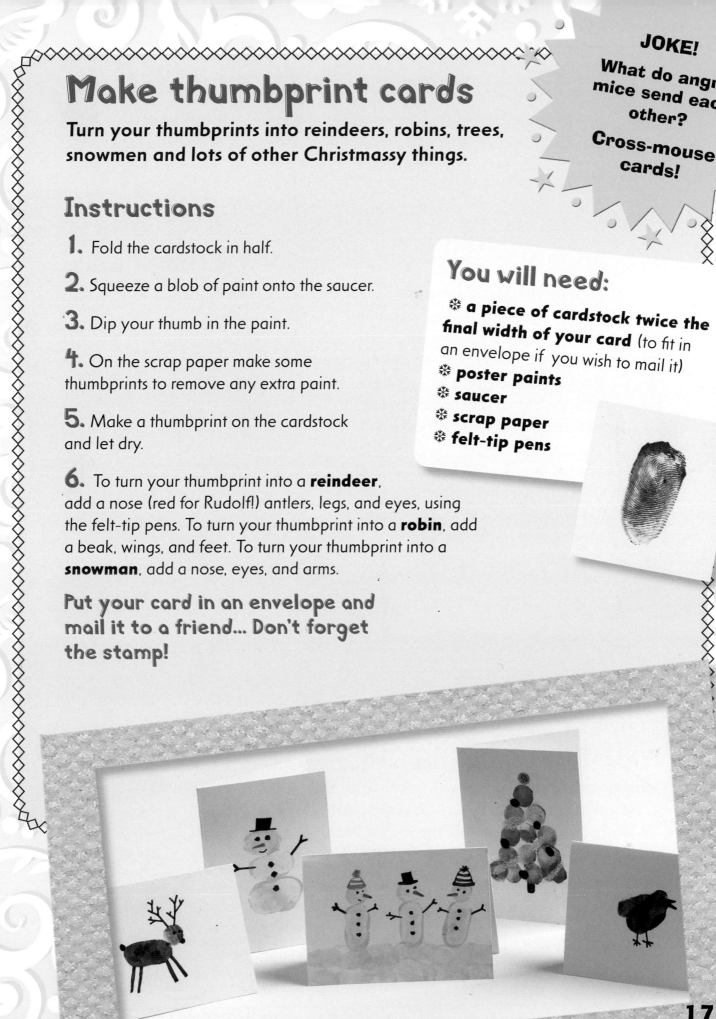

Christmas Decorations

Christmas decorations — twinkly lights and baubles, tinsel and garlands, wreaths and trees — all add a touch of sparkle to the Christmas celebrations.

Christmas trees

It is thought that Martin Luther, a German monk, decorated the first Christmas tree. He was walking in a forest one evening and saw the stars sparkling through the trees. He took home a small fir tree and decorated it with lighted candles to remind his congregation of heaven.

The Christmas tree was made popular in the United Kingdom by Prince Albert, the German husband of Queen Victoria. The tradition soon spread to many countries.

The real meaning of Christmas

Angels are an important part of the Christmas story. It was an angel who appeared to Mary to tell her that she was going to have a baby. Another angel found the shepherds in the field to tell them that Jesus had been born. That is why angels are put on top of the Christmas tree.

The symbol of a star is everywhere at Christmas. Putting a bright star in the sky was God's way of showing to the world that his son had been born on Earth. It was this bright star that the three kings followed to find Jesus.

Make an angel decoration

You will need:

- ❅ **a piece of paper 16 ½ in. x 7 in.** (42 cm x 18 cm)
- ❅ **ribbon**
- ❅ **glue**
- ❅ **colored paper**
- ❅ **felt-tip pens**
- ❅ **a scissors**

Instructions

1. Fold over **½ in.** (1 ⅓ cm) of the paper. Turn it over and fold back the same width. Keep doing this until you have a fan shape.

2. Using the ribbon, tie the fan tightly together 1 inch (2.5 cm) from the top.

3. Open the fan out at the top and bottom.

4. Cut out a pair of wings. Glue onto the back of the fan.

5. Cut out a head shape. Draw on a face. Attach to the top of the fan.

6. Glue a loop of ribbon to the back of the head.

Hang your angel on the Christmas tree.

Make a glittery bauble

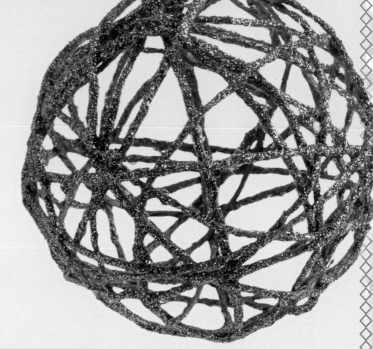

You will need:
* a ball of string
* balloon
* a scissors
* equal amounts of white glue and water mixed together in a bowl
* a cup
* a pin
* glitter
* ribbon

Instructions

1. Blow the balloon up to the size you want your finished bauble to be. Tie the end.
2. Unwind a quarter of the ball of string.
3. Put the string into the bowl with the glue and water. Leave the end of the string hanging over the edge of the bowl so that you can find it later.

4. With your hand, squish the glue onto the string.
5. Put the balloon into the bowl. Wind the string round the balloon until it looks like the one in the picture.
6. Balance it on top of the cup and leave it overnight to dry.
7. Using the pin, burst the balloon. Pull it out from inside the string ball.
8. Brush the bauble with glue.
9. Sprinkle with glitter. Leave to dry.
10. Thread a piece of ribbon through one of the holes.

Hang the finished bauble on the Christmas tree.

Make popcorn garlands

You will need:

❄ popped plain popcorn
❄ 5 feet (1.5 m) of embroidery thread
❄ a needle

Instructions

1. Thread the needle with the embroidery thread. Push the threaded needle through a piece of popcorn.

2. Slide the popcorn down, near to the end of the thread. Knot the embroidery threads together above the popcorn.

3. Keep threading the popcorn onto the thread until it is nearly full. Tie a knot round the last piece of popcorn.

Loop the garland onto the branches of the Christmas tree.

JOKE!

What do you get if you eat too many Christmas decorations?

You get tinsel-itis!

ECO TIP: Christmas for the birds

After Christmas this garland can be draped round a tree in the garden. The birds and squirrels will enjoy their Christmas treat!

Make stained-glass window cookies

Going to church is one of the traditions of Christmas. People sing carols and think about the Christmas story. Some churches are decorated for Christmas, and with the winter light shining through the stained-glass windows, it can feel very special.

The center of these cookies looks just like the stained glass in a church window. They make lovely Christmas decorations because, as they move, they catch the light and sparkle.

You will need:
* ❄ 2 small plastic bags
* ❄ a rolling pin
* ❄ a mixing bowl
* ❄ a pastry board
* ❄ a sieve
* ❄ heart-shaped cookie cutter
* ❄ star-shaped cookie cutter
* ❄ smaller cookie cutters for the middle cutout
* ❄ baking tray
* ❄ a straw
* ❄ thin ribbon
* ❄ plastic wrap

Ingredients:
* ❄ 1 c. (225g) plain flour
* ❄ a pinch of salt
* ❄ ½ c. (125g) sugar
* ❄ ½ c. (125g) butter
* ❄ 1tsp vanilla extract
* ❄ 1 egg, beaten
* ❄ 1Tbsp plain flour (for rolling)
* ❄ 6 red hard candies
* ❄ 6 green hard candies

Instructions

1. Put the red and green candies into separate plastic bags. Tap the bags gently with a rolling pin until the candies are crushed into small pieces.

2. Sieve the cup of flour and pinch of salt into a mixing bowl. Rub in the butter.

3. Add the sugar, vanilla extract, and beaten egg and mix together.

4. Sieve the tablespoonful of flour onto the pastry board and turn the mixture onto it. Knead the mixture together with your hands until it is nice and smooth. Wrap the ball of mixture in plastic wrap and put it in the fridge for 30 minutes.

Preheat the oven to 350°F (180°C)

5. Roll out the mixture to about ¼ inch (⅔ cm). Use the star and heart cookie cutters to cut out as many shapes as you can.

6. Using the smaller cutters, cut out a small shape from the middle of each cookie.

7. Cut out a hole at the top of each shape using a straw.

8. Put the shapes on a baking tray. Sprinkle the crushed candies into the center holes.

9. Bake for about 10–12 minutes or until the cookies are golden brown and the candies have melted. Let the cookies cool completely before you take them off the baking tray.

10. Thread a piece of ribbon through the small hole.

Tie the cookies on the Christmas tree.

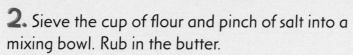

Who is Santa Claus?

A Santa Claus figure exists all over the world, but goes by different names. He may be called Father Christmas, Papa Noël, or Kris Kringle. All are versions of St. Nicholas — but who is he?

St. Nicholas

St. Nicholas is the patron saint of children. Nicholas was born in AD 270 and was brought up as a Christian in Greece. His parents died while he was still young. He used the money they left him to help people who were suffering in some way. He dedicated his life to God and was made a bishop while he was still quite young. People were not allowed to be Christians at the time and so he was put into prison and then sent away to live in exile in another land.

Christmas stockings

There are several stories about St. Nicholas's good works. In those days, to be able to marry, a young woman had to have a sum of money to offer her husband-to-be's family. This was called a dowry. Nicholas knew of three girls who did not have a dowry. He dropped a purse of gold down the chimney for them. The purse landed in a stocking drying by the fire! And so the tradition of hanging up a Christmas stocking ready to receive presents was created.

Santa Claus' helpers

A popular Christmas story is "Rudolf the Red-nosed Reindeer." Rudolph and eight other reindeer are said to pull Santa Claus' sleigh as he delivers gifts on Christmas Eve night. The reindeer names are:

**Dasher   Dancer   Prancer   Vixen   Comet
Cupid   Donner   Blitzen   Rudolph**

What does he look like?

In the 1860s, an American artist called Thomas Nast drew a picture for *Harper's Magazine*. This illustration showed Santa Claus as a jolly old man with a long white beard wearing robes trimmed with fur. This is the Santa Claus we recognize today.

JOKE!
What do you get if you cross Santa Claus with a detective?

Santa Clues!

Dear Santa Claus . . .

Lots of children write to Santa Claus each year to tell him that they have been good and what they would like for Christmas. Some people believe that he lives in Lapland, Finland, or in the North Pole. If you want to write to him, use this address:

Santa Claus Post Office
45 North Kringle Place
Santa Claus, IN 47579

Or, have an adult help you send an email at this website: www.aletter4santa.com

The real meaning of Christmas

Santa Claus is not part of Jesus's Christmas story, but he reminds us that Christmas is a time to be kind to everyone. We give presents at Christmastime to be kind and generous. Santa Claus is kind to children who have been good. Remember that when you open your presents.

All Wrapped Up!

Christmas gifts are traditionally wrapped in paper. Making your own wrapping paper and packaging can make a gift very personal and special. Try one of these simple ideas.

Make a muffin jar

You will need:

* a large glass jar with a lid
* dry ingredients for making a muffin:
  - 1¼ c. (300g) self-raising flour
  - 2 tsp baking powder
  - 2 tsp ground cinnamon
  - 2 tsp ground nutmeg
  - ½ c. (140g) mixed dried fruits
  - ⅓ c. (100g) sugar
* printed or handwritten recipe
* ribbons, stickers or fabric to decorate the jar

Recipe for muffins:

1. Place the contents of this jar into a large mixing bowl.

2. Make a well in the center and add 2 beaten eggs, 1¼ c. (300mL) milk, ⅓ c. (100g) butter and mix together into a batter.

3. Divide the mixture into muffin cases and bake at 350°F (180°C) for 18 minutes.

Instructions

1. Put the dry ingredients into the jar in layers. Press each layer down so that the layers stay separate.

2. Put the lid on the jar and attach a copy of the recipe.

3. Decorate the jar any way you like.

Make a promise box

Instructions

1. Decorate a small box with lots of Christmas pictures and colored paper. You could cut out Christmas shapes like stars or trees. You could also overlap the pictures to cover the whole box.

2. Write promise messages on slips of paper. You can make a promise box for anyone – just make sure the promises are things you know they would like (and that you can keep!). The person who receives the box can use their Christmas promises at any time.

Sample promises for Mom or Dad: **I promise to make my bed every day. I promise to walk the dog. I promise to clean the car.**

Make sponge print wrapping paper

You will need:
* large sheet of plain paper
* a sponge * felt-tip pen
* a scissors * a plate
* poster paint * scrap paper

Instructions

1. Use the felt-tip pen to draw a simple Christmas shape onto the sponge. A star, a heart, or a Christmas tree all work well.

2. Cut out the shape.

3. Squeeze a blob of paint onto the plate.

4. Dab the sponge shape into the paint. Make sure all the shape is covered.

5. On the scrap paper make some trial prints to remove any extra paint from the sponge.

6. Print the shape all over the paper.

7. Leave to dry.

8. To add another shape or color to the wrapping paper design, cut out a second shape from the sponge and repeat the process with a different colored paint.

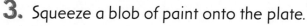

Christmas Food

Eating delicious food at Christmastime is part of the celebration in many countries.

Poland

Poland is a mostly Catholic country and Christmas Eve is a day when meat is not allowed. It is traditional not to eat until the first star is seen in the sky. Then people enjoy a special meal. This might include beetroot soup, mushroom ravioli, pasta dumplings filled with either cheese and potato or cabbage and mushroom, and fish dishes made with carp or herring.

Australia

As Christmas in Australia falls in the middle of the summer and because the weather is very hot, the Christmas meal is often served cold. Popular dishes include seafood such as prawns and lobster, as well as cold chicken or turkey, served with salads.

Jamaica

In Jamaica, Christmas fruitcake is very popular. The fruits for the cake are soaked in wine and rum for months before Christmas.

Spain

Most people in Spain go to Midnight Mass. It is called the "Mass of the Rooster" because a rooster is supposed to have crowed the night that Jesus was born. Most families eat their main Christmas meal on Christmas Eve before the service. The traditional Spanish Christmas dinner is turkey stuffed with savory truffles.

United States

The US has lots of different cultures and traditions, and Christmas varies from state to state. However, many of the Christmas customs are similar to those in the United Kingdom. The main Christmas meal might be roast turkey but, as that is eaten at the Thanksgiving meal in November, some people prefer to have a different meat at Christmas. Desserts include pumpkin pie (left), fudge, and Christmas cookies.

United Kingdom

Christmas dinner in the UK traditionally includes a roast turkey with roast potatoes and vegetables—usually lots of Brussels sprouts! For dessert it's usual to have a Christmas pudding, which is made of sweet, rich fruit and spices—sometimes covered in brandy and served flaming.

France

The French eat a Yule log-shaped cake called the *bûche de Noël*, which means Christmas log (see recipe on page 31). The cake is served at a late supper called *le réveillon* held after Midnight Mass on Christmas Eve.

Germany

In Germany, the main Christmas meal is traditionally roast meat. Favorite desserts and pastries are spice bars called *Lebkuchen* and fruit breads like *Christstollen* and *Stollen* (right).

Make Christmas punch

You will need:
* ❄ 16 oz. (460mL) apple juice
* ❄ 16 oz. (460mL) ginger ale
* ❄ 16 oz. (460mL) cranberry juice
* ❄ ½ c. (110g) sugar
* ❄ 2 cinnamon sticks
* ❄ orange slices
* ❄ ice cubes
* ❄ a large saucepan

Lots of people drink mulled wine or a spicy fruit punch at Christmas, usually served hot. Here's a cool alternative to enjoy.

Instructions

1. In a large saucepan, mix the apple juice, ginger ale, and cranberry juice. Stir in the sugar and add the cinnamon sticks and orange slices.

2. Ask an adult to heat everything together until the sugar has dissolved.

3. Remove the pan from the heat, and allow the punch to cool.

4. Take out the cinnamon sticks, using a utensil.

5. Pour the punch into a bowl and add some ice cubes.

6. Serve in a mug or glass.

You might want to leave a glass out for Santa Claus!

Make a Christmas log

This yummy chocolate log is similar to the *bûche de Noël* eaten in France on Christmas Eve.

Instructions

1. Beat the butter in a mixing bowl until smooth and then gradually beat in the powdered sugar and cocoa powder.

2. Cut off one end of the swiss roll at an angle. On a plate, put the end slice alongside the swiss roll to look like a branch.

3. Spread the butter mixture over the swiss roll to cover it. Make marks in the icing with a fork to make it look like tree bark. Dust with cocoa powder.

4. To make your log look like a fallen branch in a snowy wood, decorate it with a sprig of holly. Scatter with powdered sugar to look like snow.

You will need:
- ❄ a chocolate swiss roll
- ❄ ½ c. (100g) butter
- ❄ ⅔ c. (150g) powdered sugar
- ❄ 3½ Tbsp (55g) cocoa powder
- ❄ extra cocoa powder for decoration
- ❄ a mixing bowl
- ❄ a large spoon
- ❄ a knife

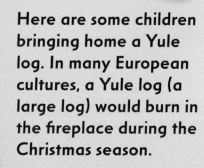

Here are some children bringing home a Yule log. In many European cultures, a Yule log (a large log) would burn in the fireplace during the Christmas season.

Make mince pies

Mince pies are a traditional Christmas food. They have been part of Christmas celebrations in the United Kingdom since Tudor times, dating back to the 1500s. In those days mince pies contained shredded meat as well as fruit and spices.

Ingredients:

❄ ⅔ c. (150g) cold butter, cut into small pieces
❄ 1½ c. (350g) plain flour
❄ cold water
❄ 1¼ c. (280g) mincemeat
❄ extra butter (to grease tins)
❄ 1 small egg, beaten
❄ powdered sugar

You will need:

❄ a large bowl
❄ a sieve
❄ a wooden spoon
❄ a teaspoon
❄ plastic wrap
❄ round cookie cutter
❄ star-shaped cookie cutter
❄ rolling pin
❄ pastry brush
❄ cupcake tray
❄ wire cooling rack

Instructions

1. Sift the flour into a large bowl.

2. Add the butter to the flour.

3. Rub the flour and butter between your fingertips until the mixture looks like fine breadcrumbs.

4. Add 12 teaspoons of cold water and mix into a ball of dough with a wooden spoon.

5. Wrap the dough in plastic wrap and put it in the fridge for 20 minutes.

Preheat the oven to 350°F (180°C)

6. Sprinkle some flour onto the work surface. Using a rolling pin, roll the dough out until it is ¼ inch thick (⅔ cm) and cut out 18 circles.

7. Using the pastry brush, brush some melted butter onto the tins.

8. Press one circle of pastry into each hole.

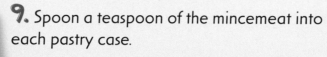

9. Spoon a teaspoon of the mincemeat into each pastry case.

10. Roll out the remaining dough and cut out star shapes to the same thickness as the circles. Place a star on top of each mince pie to make a lid.

11. Use the pastry brush to brush the stars with beaten egg.

12. Bake for 15-20 minutes, or until the pastry is golden.

13. Remove from the oven and leave the pies in the tin for 10 minutes. Then, using a knife, carefully lift the pies out onto a wire rack and leave to cool. Sift a little powdered sugar on top.

It is traditional to make a wish when you eat your first mince pie of the season.

33

Christmas Crackers

Crackers are a fun part of the celebration on Christmas Day. They are a Christmas tradition in the United Kingdom and in countries such as Australia, Canada, and South Africa.

What are Christmas crackers?

Christmas crackers are a cardboard tube covered with a twist of colored and decorated paper. Inside the inner tube are small gifts such as a paper hat, a small toy or gift, a motto or joke and a cracker snap. The cracker snap is made from two cardboard strips treated with chemicals so that when they are pulled apart they react with a loud "crack." One person holds each end of the cracker and pulls. The cracker splits apart with a bang and the gifts spill out.

Where did they come from?

It was a London pastry cook called Tom Smith who invented Christmas crackers in Victorian times. Tom spent a holiday in Paris and saw French candies wrapped in twists of colored paper. He copied the idea in England and added riddles and mottoes inside the wrappings.

When watching a log crackling in the fire one day he wondered if it would be possible to add a tiny explosion to the package. After many experiments he devised the idea of the cardboard strips treated with chemicals that are still used today.

Make your own Christmas crackers

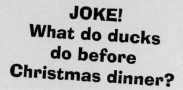

You will need:
* ❄ bright wrapping paper
* ❄ a scissors
* ❄ cardboard tube
* ❄ sticky tape
* ❄ ribbon
* ❄ jokes written on pieces of paper
* ❄ small gifts to put inside the crackers

JOKE!
What do ducks do before Christmas dinner?

Pull their Christmas quackers!

Instructions

1. Cut the cardboard tube in half.

2. Cut one of these halves in half again.

3. Lay the paper on the table. Take the larger part of the tube and place it in the middle. Put a joke and a small gift inside it.

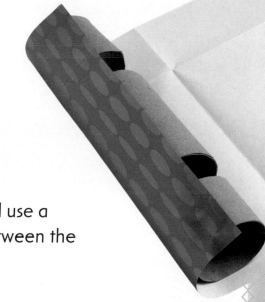

4. Put the smaller tubes at either end, leaving a small space between the tubes.

5. Roll the wrapping paper round the tubes and use a small piece of tape to hold it together. Tie in between the tubes with the ribbon.

6. Remove the two small tubes.

Pull the crackers with a friend and see who gets the gift inside!

The Three Kings

Epiphany is a Christian festival held on January 6. It celebrates the time when the three kings, also known as the wise men, visited Jesus to worship him and give him gifts. The three kings were called Caspar, Melchior, and Balthazar. They traveled from countries far away in the East to worship Jesus and to give him presents of gold, frankincense, and myrrh.

Twelfth Day

Another name for this day is "Twelfth Day" because it is the last of the Twelve Days of Christmas, which used to be one long holiday. It can feel like a sad time of year, when the Christmas decorations are taken down and Christmas is over. However in some parts of the world it is also a time to celebrate.

The Day of the Three Kings

In Mexico, children get their main presents at Epiphany, which is called "The Day of the Three Kings". The presents are left by the three kings (or Magi). A traditional food eaten at Epiphany is Three Kings Cake (right). The cake contains a figure of the baby Jesus. The person who finds the figure of baby Jesus in their piece of cake looks after him for that year.

JOKE!
What's a child's favorite king at Christmas?

A stocKING!

The Festival of the Three Magic Kings

In Spain, Epiphany is called "The Festival of the Three Magic Kings." Children are given some presents on Christmas Day, but most are opened at Epiphany. On the evening before Epiphany they leave out their shoes to be filled with gifts.

The Festival of the Kings

Epiphany in France is known as *la Fête des Rois* (the Festival of the Kings). People like to eat a flat almond cake called a *Galette des Rois*. The cake has a toy crown inside and sometimes has a gold paper crown on top.

ECO TIP

Use any left-over scraps of wrapping paper, ribbon, tags and cards to decorate small boxes like the ones the three kings gave to Jesus. Use them to put gifts in later in the year.

Christmas Play Script

Lots of schools put on a play of the Christmas story and here is a script to help you perform your own. Included are some suggestions of carols you may want to sing and get your audience to join in.

Costumes

Finding costumes for the play is a good chance to get creative with what you have around you. You can use old bed sheets as robes, with a belt round the waist. Kitchen towels make great headdresses for Joseph and the shepherds, with a piece of wool or cord around the head to keep them in place. You can make your own crowns for the kings from paper or cardboard, use tinsel for the angel's halo and decorate a pair of cardboard angel wings.

Cast:
Narrator
Joseph
Mary
Angel
Innkeepers
Shepherds
Three Kings

Scene 1: Mary's house in Nazareth

Narrator: Mary and Joseph lived in a village called Nazareth in Galilee. They were engaged to be married when one day an extraordinary thing happened.

Mary: Aaaargggggghhh!

Angel: Mary, there's no need to be scared—I'm not going to hurt you.

Mary: What do you want?

Angel: I'm here to give you a message from God. It's good news. You're going to have a baby. The baby is to be called Jesus and he is the Son of God.

Mary: A baby! No. That's not possible.

Angel: Believe me it is. Your cousin Elizabeth is going to have a child too.

Mary: But she can't have a child. She is too old.

Angel: It is God's will, Mary. God can make anything happen.

Mary: But why me?

Angel: God has chosen you, Mary. You are very special.

Narrator: When the angel had gone Mary visited her cousin Elizabeth and told her what had happened. The angel was right. Both Mary and Elizabeth were expecting babies. Mary was excited, but frightened, too. At first Joseph didn't believe her.

Joseph: This can't be true—it's too incredible to believe!

Narrator: But then the angel appeared to Joseph as well and told him that it was true. Mary and Joseph got married. Just before the baby was due to be born, Joseph ran in with more news.

Joseph: Mary, I've just heard that the Romans are organizing a census and we have to go back to Bethlehem to be counted and pay our taxes.

Mary: When?

Joseph: Now! If we don't go we will be fined or sent to prison.

Mary: But I can't walk all that way! It's seventy miles—it will take weeks.

Joseph: I'll get a donkey for you to ride on. I know it won't be comfortable but it's the best I can do.

Mary: I'm sure God will make sure that nothing awful happens to us. I'll start packing.

Narrator: So Joseph went to find a donkey and Mary began to pack the things that she would need when the baby was born.

Carol 1 – "Once in Royal David's City"

Scene 2: Bethlehem

Mary: At last—I'm so tired Joseph—Where are we going to sleep?

Joseph: I'll find a room for the night.

Narrator: Mary sat and waited while Joseph tried to find them a room.

First Innkeeper: Sorry, full up!

Second Innkeeper: We're full. There's a census going on you know.

Narrator: But he couldn't find a room anywhere.

Joseph: I've tried everywhere but they're all full. This is our last hope.

Third Innkeeper: Sorry, no room.

Joseph: Please—we'll take anything. My wife is about to have a baby and we're desperate.

Third Innkeeper: I don't have any rooms but there is a stable around the back if you want to get inside out of the cold.

Narrator: So Mary and Joseph made their way to the stable and Joseph made Mary as comfortable as he could. That night Mary's baby was born. She wrapped him in the clothes she had brought with her and they laid him in the manger that was used for the cattle's straw.

Scene 3: A field just outside Bethlehem

Carol 2 – "While Shepherds Watched Their Flocks"

Narrator: In a field just outside Bethlehem, the local shepherds were sitting around a fire while their sheep grazed nearby. It was just an ordinary night, and then…

Shepherds 1-3 in unison: Aaaaarggggghhh!

Angel: No need to be frightened. God wants you to know that in Bethlehem tonight a baby was born. His name is Jesus and he will be a great king.

Shepherd 1: Why are you telling us? We are poor, he won't want to see us!

Angel: He is poor as well. He has been born in a stable but he will grow up and bring peace to all people.

Shepherd 1: Should we go and see if it's true?

Shepherd 2: Good idea! Let's go.

Shepherd 1: Wait a minute. We should take him a present.

Shepherd 2: We don't have anything to give him.

Shepherd 3: We could take him a lamb . . .

Shepherd 2: That's a great idea.

Narrator: The shepherds chose a lamb and then went to Bethlehem where they found Mary and Joseph in the stable with the baby Jesus.

Scene 4: The stable

Shepherd 1: This is just as the angel told us. He really is poor.

Shepherd 2: ... but he will be a great king.

Shepherd 3: ... and he will bring peace to all people.

Narrator: The shepherds knelt in front of the manger and offered the lamb as their gift to Jesus.

Scene 5: On the road to Bethlehem

Narrator: Somewhere in the East, three kings had been watching the night sky. They saw a bright star appear. It was the sign they had been waiting for. They knew that it meant the birth of a new king and they set out to find him.

First King: (looking shocked) The star is right over that stable!

Second King: Let's go and look inside.

Third King: Here he is. This baby is the new king who will bring peace to all people on Earth.

Narrator: The kings knelt in front of the manger and gave Jesus gifts.

First King: Gold!

Second King: Frankincense!

Third King: Myrrh!

Three Kings in unison: Peace on Earth and goodwill to all!

Final carol – "O Come, All Ye Faithful"

Christmas Quiz

How much do you really know about Christmas? Be a Christmas know all (Noël! Get it?!) and teach your friends lots of interesting Christmas facts. All the answers are somewhere in this book.

❄ Where did Mary and Joseph go to be counted?

❄ What are the names of the three kings?

❄ Who invented the Christmas cracker?

❄ When does Advent begin?

❄ When is Epiphany?

❄ What presents did the three kings give to Jesus?

❄ Who drew the first picture of Santa Claus in his robes with a white beard?

❄ Who brought the tradition of the Christmas tree to the UK?

❄ On what date is St. Lucia's Day?

❄ Who sent the first Christmas card?

Find the stocking challenge!

There are ten Christmas stockings like this one hidden in this book.

HOW MANY CAN YOU FIND?

Christmas numbers!

The missing Christmas numbers on page 12 are:
- **Twelve** days of Christmas
- **Five** candles in an advent crown
- **Three** wise men
- Santa Claus has **nine** reindeer

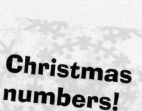

Index